IMO OLYMPIAD WORKBOOK

4

SOF INTERNATIONAL MATHEMATICS OLYMPIAD 2023-24

SANAGE EDITORIAL BOARD

Paperback: 978-811937378-9

Any references to historical events, real people, or real places are used fictitiously. Names, characters, and places are products of the author's imagination.

Printed by:

Sanage Publishing House LLP
Mumbai, India

sanagepublishing@gmail.com

Contents

NUMBER SENSE

**DO YOU KNOW
WHAT TOPICS WE WILL COVER IN THIS CHAPTER?**

Yes! the topics are;
* Numerals and numbers names of more than 4 - digit numbers
* Place value in the Indian and International system
* Roman numbers upto 1000
* Estimation in nearest ten's, hundred's, thousand's
* Formation of a number using given information
* Expanded form
* Ascending-Descending order
* Word problems

MATHEMATICAL REASONING

1. 1 thousand =____.

   A) 10 tens   B) 10 lakh   C) 100 tens   D) 100 tens

DIRECTION (2-3): Using 8, 1, 4, 3, 5 digits only once, answer the following questions.

2. Smallest five digit number is ___.

   A) 13458   B) 14584   C) 14458   D) 13548

3. Largest five digit number having 4 at hundred's place ___.

   A) 85431   B) 84513   C) 81435   D) 14458

4. The difference between the place value of '2' and '6' in 42965 is ___.

   A) 1490   B) 1940   C) 1049   D) 1409

5. **Select the odd one out.**

   A) 100 tens   B) 10 tens   C) 1 thousand   D) 1000 ones

6. **Expanded from of 48269 is ___.**

   A) 4000+800+200+60+9   B) 40000+8000+200+60+9

   C) 4000+800+60+9   D) 4000+800+60+200+9

7. **The ascending order of 6515, 6530, 6120, 6530 is ___**

   A) 6813, 6515, 6530, 6120

   B) 6120, 6515, 6530, 6813

   C) 6813, 6530, 6515, 6120

   D) 6120, 6530, 6813, 6515

8. **Place Value of 3 in 93, 365 is ___.**

   A) 300   B) 3000   C) 3   D) 30

9. **10 lakh = ___.**

   A) 100 million   B) 1 million   C) 10 million   D) 100 million

10. **Eighty one thousand five hundred seventy is same as___.**

    A) 81500   B) 81570   C) 81507   D) 80157

11. **40602 = ___ thousands + 60 tens + 2 ones.**

    A) 4   B) 40   C) 400   D) 40000

12. **The number on the basket shows the best estimate of which of the following number of flowers?**

    A) 145   B) 200   C) 175   D) 250

13. **Which of the following statements is INCORRECT?**

    A) Q is the largest of all the other numbers.

B) P is the smallest of all the other numbers.

C) R is the smallest of all the other numbers.

D) S is the second largest of all the other numbers.

8409	P
8499	Q
8470	R
8490	S

14. Which of the following is meaningless?

A) IXVI   B) IXIX   C) XXI   D) IXV

DIRECTION (15-16): using the given table and answer the following questions.

Roman Numerals	I	V	X	L	C	D	M
Hindu Arabic Numbers	1	5	10	50	100	500	1000

15. LD =____

A) 50 - 100   B) 500 - 50   C) 1000 - 5   D) 200-100

16. CVV =____

A) 90   B) 105   C) 155   D) 110

17. What is 63428 rounded to the nearest thousands?

A) 63400   B) 64000   C) 63420   D) 60000

18. Which should not be placed in the box to have the number in order from the greatest to the least?

| 8843 | 3623 | ? | 1239 |

A) 2321   B) 2980   C) 5740   D) 3513

19. Which of the following is same as 7504?

A) 700+50+4   B) 7+5+0+4

C) 7000+50+4   D) 7000+500+4

20. **74392 is 74390 when rounded off to the nearest___.**

A) Tens   B) Thousand   C) Ten thousand   D) Hundred

EVERYDAY MATHEMATICS

21. **A town has a population of 65492. Rounded off the population 65492 to the nearest hundreds.**

A) 64500   B) 65500   C) 66500   D) 65400

22. **If there are 34523 seats in auditorium P, 34570 seats in auditorium Q and 18535 seats in auditorium R, then in which auditorium the number of seats were most?**

A) R   B) P   C) Q   D) Can't be determined

23. **The ABC company estimated the cost to build a new cricket ground which is Rupees fourty nine thousand. What is this number in numeral form?**

A) 40900   B) 49000   C) 40009   D) 40090

24. **The given picture shows a copy of four different story book. The number under each magazine is the total number of copies of the magazine sold last year.**

63210   86270   24693   81266

Which story book sold a number of copies that has a 6 in the ten thousand's place ?

A) My Little Blue Story Book   B) My Little Yellow Story book
C) My Little Green Story book   D) My Little Red Story Book

25. **Nandita was solving a mathematics question. She calculated**

that there are thirty nine thousand six hundred seconds in a day. Help her to write this number in numeral form?

A) 30096   B) 30960   C) 39600   D) 39606

ACHIEVERS SECTION (HOT)

26. Which of the following statements is CORRECT?

A) Symbols V, L, D can be subtracted while writing roman numerals.

B) Symbol I cannot be subtracted from V and X only once.

C) Symbol X can be subtracted from L

D) None of these

27. Match the following.

Column 1   Column 2

P. 876452   (1) largest 5-digit number

Q. 99999   (2) Place value of 1 if 1000

R. 781548   (3) 100039 when rounded off to nearest 100

S. 100000   (4) Successor of 876451

A) P - (4), Q - (1), R - (2), S - (3)

B) P - (3), Q - (2), R - (1), S - (4)

C) P - (4), Q - (3), R - (2), S - (1)

D) P - (3), Q - (2), R - (4), S - (3)

28. Radhika's clues about her mystery number are shown in the writing pad. What is Radhika's mystery number?

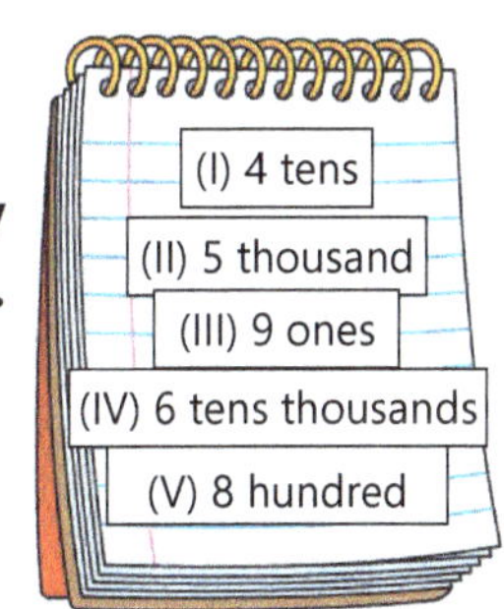

A) 54986

B) 59486

C) 54968

D) 59468

29. **P, Q, R and S are 5-digit numbers, each having the digit 8 only once and in the place shown, None of the other digits are known.**

P) | | 8 | | | | Q) | 8 | | | | |

R) | | | 8 | | | S) | | | | 8 | |

Which of the following statements is INCORRECT about P, Q, R and S?

A) S is at tens among the four numbers.

B) P is at thousand place among the four numbers.

C) Q is the smallest among the four numbers.

D) R is at hundred place among the four numbers.

30. **Compare and fill the boxes using >,< or =**

a) CCVI [ ] CC

b) LV [ ] XC

c) LXV [ ] LXX

	(a)	(b)	(c)
A)	=	<	<
B)	<	>	=
C)	>	<	<
D)	>	<	>

CHAPTER 2

COMPUTATION OPERATIONS

DO YOU KNOW WHAT TOPICS WE WILL COVER IN THIS CHAPTER?

Yes! the topics are;
* Addition and subtraction upto 5-digit numbers
* Estimated sum and diffrence by rounding off
* Sum and differences of roman numbers
* Multiplication of 3-digit numbers with 1, 2, 3-digit numbers
* Ezsy method to multiply by multiples of 10
* Estimated multiplication by rounding off
* Division of upto 5-digit numbers with 1, 2-digit numbers
* Estimated Division by rounding off
* Properties of sum, defferences, product and division
* Factor and multiples, comman factor and multiples
* Highest Common Factor (HCF) and Least Comman Multiples (LCM)
* Prime factors of numbers
* Word problems, unitary method to solve problems

MATHEMATICAL REASONING

1. Which of the following is true?

A) 18 x 78 = 78 x (12+7)   B) 18 x 78=(18 x 7) x (18 x 8)

C) 18 x 78=(71+8) x 18   D) 18 x 78=(18 x 1) x 78

2. Nisha arranged some circles in the pattern shown here. Which number sentences best represents her arrangements of cirles?

A) 6 + 3 = 9   B) 6 x 3 = 18

C) 6 x 6 = 12   D) 18 - 3 = 15

3. We have ▰ = 🍉 + 🍉 + 🍉 + 🍉 **and** ● = 🥕 + 🥕 + 🥕 +

If Armaan bought 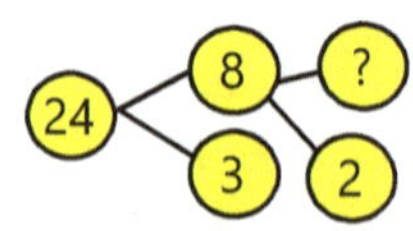 **, then how many carrots than watermelon did he buy?**

A)   B)   C)   D)

4. **Piyush has a ball of string 6 yards long. He needs 20 feet string for a project. What should Piyush do first to find out length of strings he requires? (1 yard=3 feet)**

   A) Multiply 6 by 12   B) Multiply 20 by 6

   C) Multiply 6 by 3   D) Multiply 20 by 3

5. **Which of the following shows the common factors of 14 and 16 ?**

   A) 3 and 4   B) 2 and 3   C) 1 and 2   D) 1 and 3

6. **Product of the third multiple of 4 by 9 is __**

   A) 16   B) 108   C) 58   D) 215

7. **Vedant solved the division problem as shown. Which expression could be used to check his answer?**

   A) (687 x 2) + 1

   B) (687 x 2) + 2

   C) (687 x 2) x 1

   D) (687 x 2) x 2

$$\begin{array}{r} 687 \\ 2\overline{)1375} \\ -12 \\ \hline 17 \\ -16 \\ \hline 15 \\ -14 \\ \hline 01 \end{array}$$

8. **Deepika read a 189 stories in a week. She read same number of stories each day. How many stories did she read each day?**

   A) 25   B) 24   C) 31   D) 27

9. **Find the missing number.**

   A) 4   B) 2

   C) 3   D) 5

10. **Which of the following is 'NOT' a common of 20 and 24?**

    A) 1   B) 4   C) 5   D) 2

11. **Anand bought 4 boxes of red roses and 7 boxes of white roses. Each box had 11 roses in it. Which expression could he use to find the total number of roses he bought?**

    A) (11 x 4) + 7   B) (11 x 7) + 4

    C) 11 x (4 + 7)   D) 11 +(4 x 7)

12. **A traval agency paid ₹ 10010 as fare for 13 tickets to travel from Goa to Mumbai. What was the fare of one ticket?**

    A) 1050   B) 590   C) 1010   D) 770

13. **If ◯ + ◯ + ◯ + ◯ = 88 and ◯ - 5 △ - △ than the value of △ + △ + ◯ + ◯ =?**

    A) 35   B) 65   C) 46   D) 56

14. **Smallest factor of a number is___.**

    A) 0   B) 1   C) 10   D) Number itself

15. **The numbers in region (Q) shows that the number can be divided by __ both.**

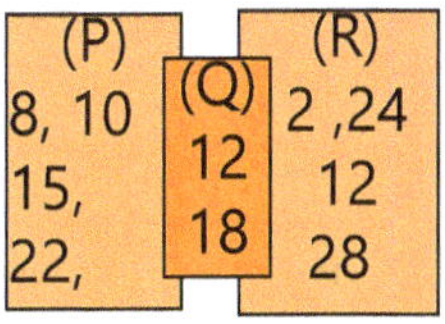

    A) 6 and 2   B) 2 and 3

    C) 4 and 5   D) 5 and 6

    (P) 8, 10 15, 22, — (Q) 12 18 — (R) 2 ,24 12 28

16. **The numbers that can be divided by both 2 and 4 can also be divided by ____**

    A) 4   B) 8   C) 6   D) 12

17. **If ▦ + ▦ + ▦ + ▦ + ▦ + ▦ = 48 rubric cube and ▦ + ◉ + ◉ + ◉ + ◉ = 220 marbles, then ◉ stands for ____.**

A) 62   B) 42   C) 30   D) 53

18. **Select the INCORRECT match.**

     A) XIV + XIX =33   B) VIII + LX = 68

     C) IVX + XVY =32   D) XXX +XXXIV = 64

19. **Think of a number. Multiply it by 14. Add 5. Multiply by 2. Subtract 9. Divide by 13. The result is 13. What is the number?**

     A) 4   B) 9   C) 6   D) 20

20. **If** $\square + \square + \square + \square + \square$ **= 1050 and 850 –** $\square$ **=** $\bigcirc$ **, then the value of** $\bigcirc$ **–** $\square$ **=?**

     A) 1020   B) 250   C) 430   D) 670

EVERYDAY MATHEMATICS

21. **There were 4236 Girls and 3489 boys in a playground. 2341 childrens left the playground. How many childrens remained in the playground?**

     A) 5122   B) 5384   C) 5800   D) 6245

22. **On March Minal run 1011 km. on April she run 476 km and on May she run 429 km. Approximately, how many kms did she run in the three months?**

     A)1786   B) 1916 km   C) 1500 km   D) 1990 km

23. **Palak bought 5 boxes of cupcakes for a birthday party. There were 20 cakes in each box. How many cupcakes did she buy altogether?**

     A) 110   B) 100   C) 150   D) 199

24. **Karan read 25 stories during his school reading program. In order to reach his goal of 95 stories, how many more stories does he need to read?**

A) 45   B) 55   C) 70   D) 65

25. **A library has 222 racks of books. If each rack holds 295 books, them find the total number of books in the library.**

A) 66,145   B) 65,490   C) 66,850   D) 60,400

ACHIEVERS SECTION (HOT)

26.  = ₹ 1280

 = ₹ 620

 = ₹ 140

 = ________.

A) 1029   B) 860   C) 880   D) 3200

27. **Match the following.**

Column-I	Column-II
I. When number A is multiplied by 10 and then divided by 8, the result is 270. Then A is	P. 1632
II. There are 48 crates of mangoes. Each crate contains 34 mangoes. Number of apples altogether are	Q. 324
III Subtract 3897 from the sum of 4867 and 20880	R. 216

IV The product of third multiple of 9 with 12 is   S. 21850

A) (I) – P, (II) – Q, (III) – R, (IV) – S

B) (I) – R, (II) – P, (III) – S, (IV) – Q

C) (I) – R, (II) – P, (III) – Q, (IV) – S

D) (I) – R, (II) – S, (III) – P, (IV) – Q

28. **Each letter represents a different digit. The same letter represents the same digit. The digits P and Q respectively are ___.**

A) 3, 4 B) 2, 3

C) 5, 4 D) 4, 3

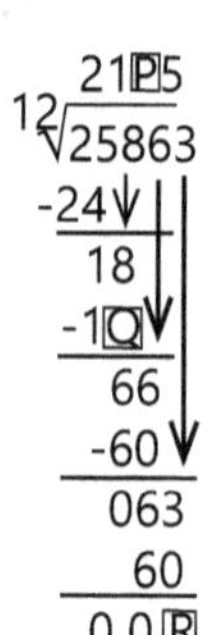

29. **Find P - Q +R**

A) 8

B) 6

C) 4

D) 9

30. **Identify it.**

- All my digits are different

- The one's digit is smallest than thousand's digit and hundred's digit s largest than ten's digit.

- I am a 5 digit number.

- They add up to 30

A) 85575   B) 72439   C) 84693   D) 93520

CHAPTER 3

FRACTIONS

DO YOU KNOW WHAT TOPICS WE WILL COVER IN THIS CHAPTER?

Yes! the topics are;
* Fraction of shaded and unshaded parts
* Simplifying fraction in its simplest form
* Equivalent fractions
* Comparing fractions (Greater or smallest). Arranging fractions in ascending and descending order
* Convert improperfraction into mixed fraction and vice versa
* Fraction representing part of a whole
* Addition subtraction, multiplication and division of fractions with fractions having same denominator
* Word problem

MATHEMATICAL REASONING

1. **What is the fraction used to represents the shaded parts?**

   A) $\frac{2}{4} + \frac{3}{4}$ B) $\frac{1}{4} + \frac{4}{4}$

   C) $\frac{5}{4} + \frac{5}{4}$ D) $\frac{2}{4} + \frac{4}{4}$

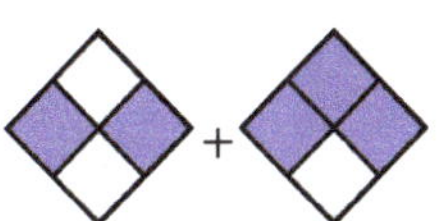

2. **By how much is $\frac{17}{15}$ greater than $\frac{8}{15}$?**

   A) $\frac{15}{15}$ B) $\frac{9}{15}$ C) $\frac{25}{15}$ D) $\frac{20}{15}$

3. **$3\frac{5}{6}$ is same as ___**

   A) $\frac{23}{6}$ B) $\frac{29}{6}$ C) $\frac{14}{6}$ D) $\frac{20}{5}$

4. Which of the following options will replace '*' if $\dfrac{4}{6} - \dfrac{*}{18}$?

   A) 12   B) 8   C) 19   D) 5

5. How many one-forths will make one whole?

   A) 4   B) 6   C) 15   D) 7

6. $\dfrac{12}{21}$ is same as ___

   A) $\dfrac{5}{8}$ B) $\dfrac{4}{7}$ C) $\dfrac{7}{4}$ D) $\dfrac{8}{7}$

7. If y- $\dfrac{9}{15}$ - $\dfrac{5}{15}$, then y ___

   A) $\dfrac{20}{15}$ B) $\dfrac{18}{15}$ C) $\dfrac{14}{15}$ D) $\dfrac{2}{15}$

8. The sum of shaded fractions are of ⬡ and ⬡ is ___

   A) $\dfrac{5}{8}$ B) $\dfrac{2}{4}$ C) $\dfrac{4}{4}$ D) $\dfrac{8}{2}$

9. Which of the following set of fractions are in asending order?

   A) $\dfrac{12}{12}, \dfrac{8}{12}, \dfrac{4}{12}, \dfrac{16}{12}, \dfrac{11}{12}$ B) $\dfrac{5}{4}, \dfrac{8}{4}, \dfrac{11}{4}, \dfrac{14}{4}, \dfrac{18}{4}$

   C) $\dfrac{18}{4}, \dfrac{13}{4}, \dfrac{9}{4}, \dfrac{5}{4}, \dfrac{2}{4}$ D) $\dfrac{15}{4}, \dfrac{11}{4}, \dfrac{7}{4}, \dfrac{9}{4}, \dfrac{10}{4}$

10. Which of the following options can make given number sentence true?

   $$\dfrac{11}{4} \ \square \ \dfrac{22}{8}$$

   A) <   B) =   C) >   D) -

11. 3 times of $\dfrac{25}{81}$ - ___.

A) $\dfrac{55}{25}$ B) $\dfrac{25}{27}$ C) $\dfrac{20}{27}$ D) $\dfrac{28}{22}$

12. What fraction of the figure is unshaded?

A) $\dfrac{16}{10}$ B) $\dfrac{9}{10}$

C) $\dfrac{12}{10}$ D) $\dfrac{4}{10}$

13. What fraction of the figure is unshaded?

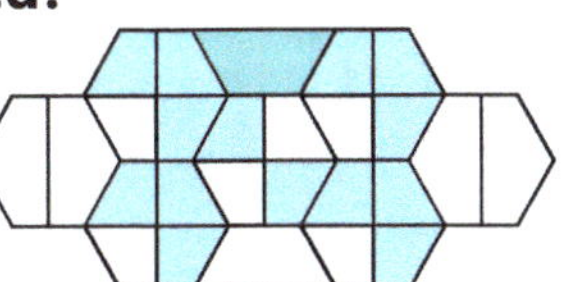

A) One quarter   B) One third

C) One half   D) Three eighths

14. What fraction of the figure is shaded?

A) $\dfrac{5}{10}$ B) $\dfrac{7}{10}$

C) $\dfrac{9}{10}$ D) $\dfrac{12}{10}$

15. The model is shaded to show which fraction?

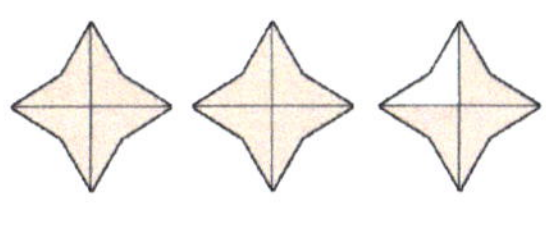

A) $2\dfrac{5}{3}$ B) $2\dfrac{3}{3}$

C) $2\dfrac{3}{4}$ D) $1\dfrac{1}{6}$

16. Which of the following shaded fraction represent less than the shaded fraction of   ?

A) 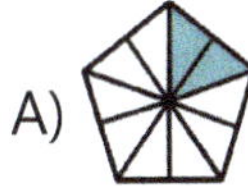   B) 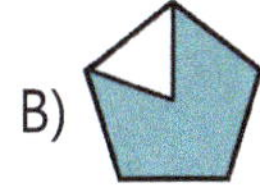   C) 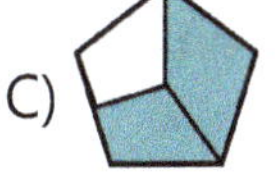   D) 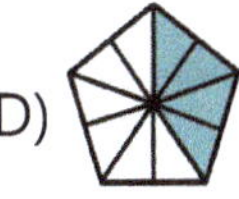

DIRECTION (17•18): Radhika has a bag with 6 green papers, 5 white papers, 3 blue papers and 6 pink papers all of the same size.

17. What fraction of papers are green?

A) $\frac{6}{20}$ B) $\frac{5}{20}$ C) $\frac{12}{20}$ D) $\frac{3}{20}$

18. **What fraction of papers are not blue?**

A) $\frac{3}{20}$ B) $\frac{17}{20}$ C) $\frac{12}{20}$ D) $\frac{6}{20}$

19. **What fraction of the figure is shaded?**

A) $\frac{7}{18}$ B) $\frac{5}{12}$

C) $\frac{7}{12}$ D) $\frac{6}{12}$

20. **The difference between $4\frac{1}{2}$ and $2\frac{1}{8}$ is _____.**

A) $2\frac{8}{10}$ B) $2\frac{3}{8}$ C) $\frac{3}{8}$ D) $4\frac{5}{8}$

EVERYDAY MATHEMATICS

21. **Mohit has some fruits cards as shown. What fraction of the cards is apple card?**

Mango	Cherry	Apple
Cherry	Mango	Apple
Apple	Bannana	Mango
Bannana	Apple	Bannana

A) $\frac{8}{12}$ B) $\frac{4}{12}$

C) $\frac{3}{12}$ D) $\frac{5}{12}$

22. **Jyoti puts the cards shown below into empty bag and mixed them up.**

$$\boxed{A}\;\boxed{C}\;\boxed{H}\;\boxed{I}\;\boxed{E}\;\boxed{V}\;\boxed{M}\;\boxed{E}\;\boxed{N}\;\boxed{T}$$

What fraction of letters on cards are vowels?

A) $\frac{2}{10}$ B) $\frac{7}{11}$ C) $\frac{4}{10}$ D) $\frac{5}{10}$

23. Dheeraj won exactly $\dfrac{3}{5}$ of the ribbons for 1st place. Which of the following could be group of ribbons Dheeraj won?

A) 

B) 

C) 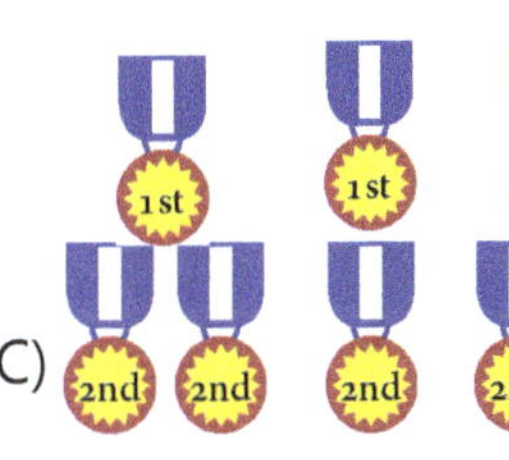

D) 

24. The given list shows the names of the students who are in the Cultural activity.

Students in the Cultural activity

Anuj	Deepti
Shubham	Aruna
Adhiraj	Shivani
Dhanush	Anandi

One student will be chosen at random. What fraction of names are starting with alphabet A?

A) $\dfrac{3}{8}$ B) $\dfrac{2}{8}$ C) $\dfrac{5}{8}$ D) $\dfrac{4}{8}$

25. Sonal bought 8 lemons out of which 2 are good. What fraction of lemons are bad?

A) $\dfrac{3}{8}$ B) $\dfrac{5}{9}$ C) $\dfrac{3}{4}$ D) $\dfrac{2}{8}$

ACHIEVERS SCETION (HOTS)

26. Shaded fraction $\dfrac{1}{4} + \dfrac{1}{12}$ is represented by which one of the following figures?

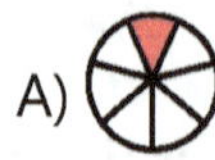 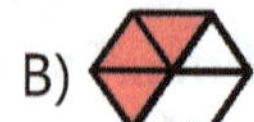 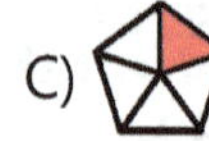 

27. **In an fruit basket, there are 4 bananas, 2 watermelons and 6 oranges. Which of the following statements about oranges is true?**

    A) Half of the fruits in basket are oranges.

    B) All fruits are oranges.

    C) More than half of the fruits in basket are oranges.

    D) None of the fruit is oranges.

28. **Which number should come in place of '?' so that sum of each arm is same?**

    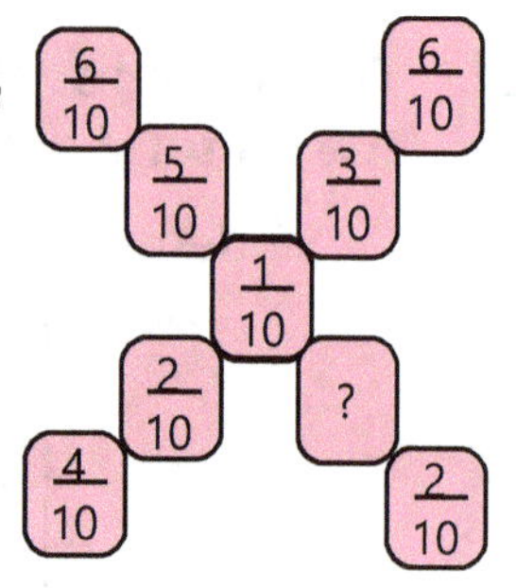

    A) $\dfrac{4}{10}$ B) $\dfrac{2}{10}$

    C) $\dfrac{8}{10}$ D) $\dfrac{5}{10}$

29. **What is the value of** 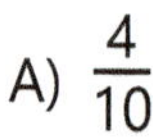 **+ ✦ + ⬡ + ★**

    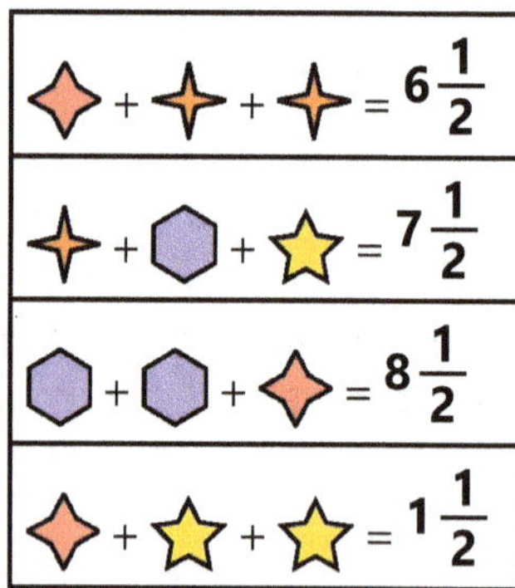

30. **A fractional part of the set of Square is shaded.**

Which of the following set of circles represents the same shaded fraction?

A) 

B) 

C) 

D) 

CHAPTER 4

LENGTH, WEIGHT, CAPACITY, TIME AND MONEY

DO YOU KNOW
WHAT TOPICS WE WILL COVER IN THIS CHAPTER?

Yes! the topics are;
* Conversation of units of time, weight, lenght, money from one unit to another
* Calculating time spent between two activities
* Relation of years, months, weeks, days, hous, minutes, seconds
* Calender Reading
* Addition and subtraction of time
* Measuring weights/lengths using weighting scale/ruler
* Comparing weights/ lengths
* Calculating money in shopping activities
* Word problems

MATHEMATICAL REASONING

1. **Divya leaves for school at 9:15 p.m. She reaches school at 10:05 p.m. How long does Divya take to reach school?**

   A) 50 mins   B) 45 mins   C) 55 mins   D) 60 mins

2. **71 km 37 m +21 km 8 m =**

   A) 9245 km   B) 902 km 45 m

   C) 92 km 450 m   D) 92 km 45 m

3. **How many 250 g rice packets are required to make 3 kg?**

   A) 12   B) 6   C) 10   D) 15

4. **If cost of 2 kg apples is ₹ 220, then what is the cost of 500g apples?**

A) ₹ 120   B) ₹ 55   C) ₹ 100   D) ₹ 60

5. The weight of each of the 2 melon is ___

A) 300 g   B) 350 g

C) 250 g   D) 200 g

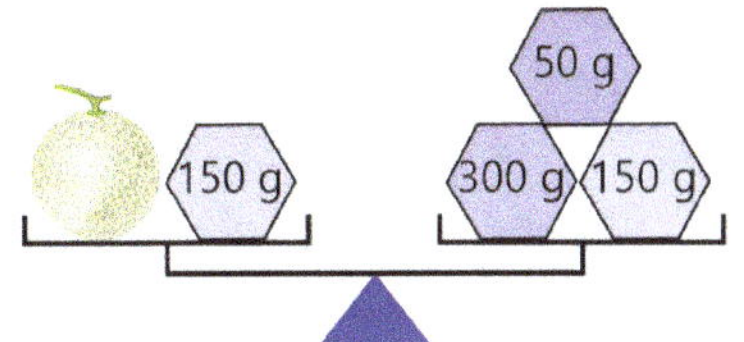

6. 1000 ml =

A) 300 ml 300 ml 300 ml   B) 250 ml 250 ml 250 ml 250 ml

C) 200 ml 200 ml 200 ml   D) 500 ml 500 ml 500 ml

7. Weight of an orange is ___g.

A) 35

B) 22

C) 25

D) 10

8. How much does  cost?

 +  +  +  = ₹ 20

 +  +  = ₹ 15

 +  +  = ₹ 20

A) ₹ 15   B) ₹ 11   C) ₹ 12   D) ₹ 10

9. **The total weight of P and Q is ___.**

A) 4100 g   B) 4300 g   C) 4800 g   D) 4900 g

10. **The following is the bill of cricket kit Aman bought from a shop. If he paid ₹ 2000, then how much will he get back?**

Bat	450
Batting gloves	250
Stumps	200
Helmet	270

A) ₹ 700   B) ₹ 830   C) ₹ 800   D) ₹ 850

11. **The mug can hold___ more ml of water than the cup.**

A) 4060 ml   B) 4600 ml

C) 460 ml   D) 4500 ml

700 ml   5 litres 300 ml

DIRECTION (12-13): Read the menu of a cafe and answer the following question.

MENU

Item	Cost	Item	Cost
Hot Coffee	20	Lassi	22
Tea	15	Cold Coffee	35
Cold Drinks	45	Butter Milk	25
Mango Shake	45	Lemon Water	20

12. **If Mona bought 1 hot coffee, 1 tea and 2 cold coffee, then how much she has to pay?**

A) ₹ 90   B) ₹ 100   C) ₹ 120   D) ₹ 105

13. **Soham has arrange a meeting with his colleagues. He bought 2 cold drinks, 1 butter milk, 2 mango shakes and 3 cold coffee. How much he has to pay?**

A) ₹ 300   B) ₹ 250   C) ₹ 310   D) ₹ 370

14. **Each item stands for a different value. The sum of each row and column is given**

What is the value  **?**

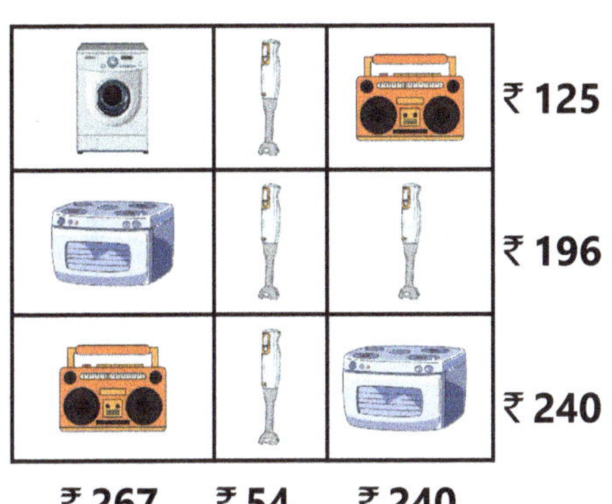

A) ₹ 14   B) ₹ 75   C) ₹ 120   D) ₹ 45

15. **Find the lightest item in the given figures.**

A) Melon   B) Glass jar   C) Jaggery powder   D)Pumkin

16. **The given pictures shows how two different groups of shapes balance a scale.**

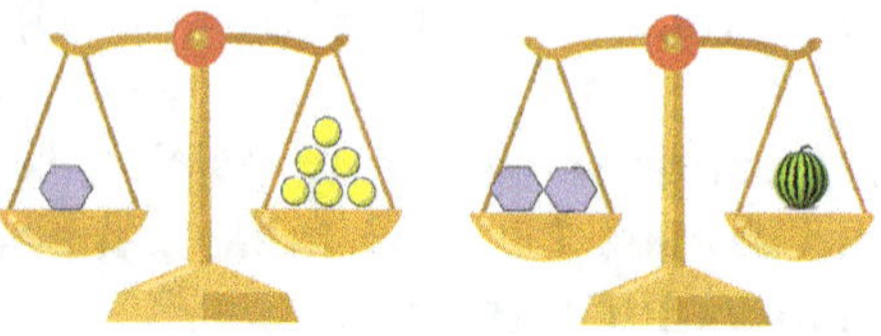

1 watermelons balances____.

A) 12 balls   B) 6 balls   C) 10 balls   D) 20 balls

17. **Rakesh wants to mark his exam date on the given calendar. He knows that his exam is four days before third monday in October 20XX.**

October 20XX						
Mon	Tue	Wed	Thu	Fri	Sat	Sun
			1	2	3	4
5	6	7	8	9	10	11
12	13	14	15	16	17	18
19	20	21	22	23	24	25
26	27	28	29	30	31	

A) Monday, October 19   B) Saturday, October 17

C) Friday, October 16   D) Thursday, October 15

18. **Sonu took 12 mins 5 secs to walk from her home to market. On her way back home. She took another route and reached home in 10 mins 22 secs. How much time did she spent by taking the longer route?**

A) 1 min 4 secs   B) 84 secs

C) 1 min 43 secs   D) Both (b) and (c)

19. **What is the weight of a**  **?**

A) 20000 kg   B) 22 kg   C) 2220 kg   D) 24000 kg

20. **Which of the following options is CORRECT?**

A) 2 L 50 ml = 1500 ml   B) 6 L 45 ml = 6450 ml

C) 5 L 20 ml = 5020 ml   D) 3 L 44 ml = 3444 ml

EVERYDAY MATHEMATICS

21. **Mr. Varma travelled 52 km 950 m by car and 980 km 40 m by train. How much distance did he travel in all?**

A) 1032 km 990 m   B) 103299 km

C) 1132 km   D) 255840 km

22. **Nandita went to shopping with her friend's at 12:25 p.m. Her mother told her to be back home in 2 hour and 35 minutes. What time does Nandita needs to be at home?**

A) 2.30 pm

B) 2.45 pm

C) 3.10 pm

D) 3.00 pm

23. **Komal went to a cafe with her friends. She bought two coffee for ₹ 120 each, 2 coldrinks for ₹ 25 each and 2 pizza. What information is needed to find the total amount Komal spent by her?**

A) The name of Komal's friends.   B) The name of the cafe.

C) Cost of a coldrink   D) Cost of a pizza

24. **A can contains 14 liters of water. A shopkeeper empties it equally into 7 bottals. Each bottal will hold___ a water.**

A) 2 L   B) 7 L   C) 5 L   D) 28 L

25. **Anjali had 35 kg 254 g of rice. She used 23 kg 622 g of it to make a dish. How much rice is left with her?**

A) 11 kg 632 g   B) 11 kg 652 g

C) 13 kg 122 g   D) 10 kg 192 g

ACHIEVERS SECTION (HOTS)

26. **If**  **respectively is**

A) 4 kg, 6 kg   B) 5 kg, 3 kg   C) 9 kg, 2 kg   D) 6 kg, 4 kg

27. **Pratiksha is practicing for a race. She uses the given map to find the possible routes. The routes must start from her school and end at home. She wants to run the shortest route. Which of the following is the best route?**

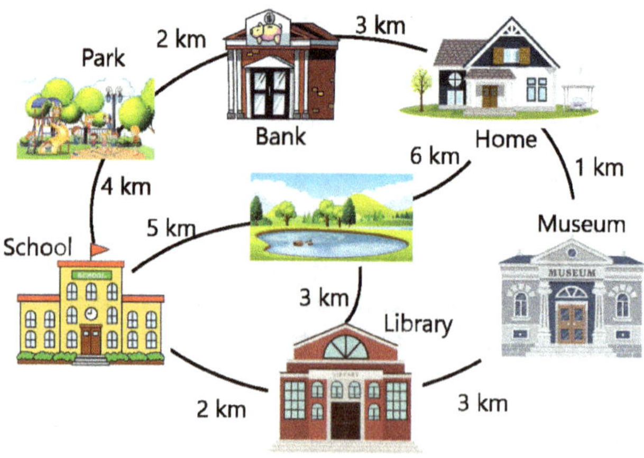

A) School- Library-Lake- Home

B) School- Lake- Home

C) School – Park-Bank-Home

D) School – Library – Museum - Home

28. **What is the value of** 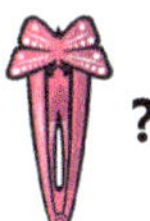 **?**

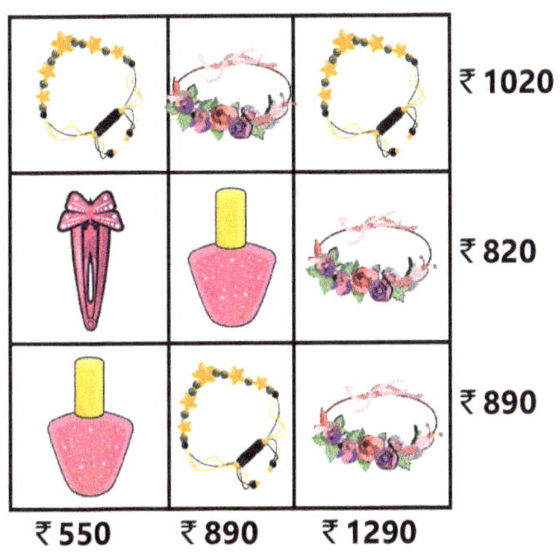

A) ₹ 150   B) ₹ 180   C) ₹ 350   D) ₹ 480

29. **Line P is twice as long as line Q. Line R is 170 cm shorter than line P. Line R is 1520 cm long, what is the total length of three lines?**

A) 8235 cm   B) 5050 cm   C) 4055 cm   D) 3470 cm

30. **If** ▯ - △ **= 10 g,** ▯ - ▬ **= 60 g and the total weight of 20** ▬ **and 10** ▯ **, and 10** △ **is 2100 g, then what is the weight of** △ **?**

A) 30 g   B) 50 g   C) 10 g   D) 80 g

GEOMETRY

DO YOU KNOW
WHAT TOPICS WE WILL COVER IN THIS CHAPTER?

Yes! the topics are;

* Counting the geometrical shapes, solides and type of lines in geometrical figures
* Identification og type of polygons
* Properties of rectangle, squares, equilateral triangles, scaleane triangles, isoscales triangle and circle
* Concept of closed and open figure/curve
* perimeter of polygons
* Concept of parallel intersecting and coinciding lines
* Identification of solid formed from the given net
* Symmetry

MATHEMATICAL REASONING

1. **The given figure contains ___ squares.**

   A) 11   B) 16

   C) 12   D) 18

2. **Which of the following dotted lines represents the line of symmetry?**

   A) EF   B) AB

   C) CD   D) GH

   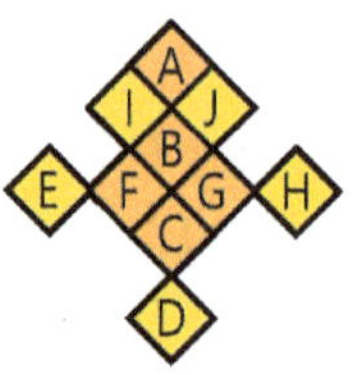

3.     are all___.

   A) Polygones   B) Triangles

   C) Quadrilaterals   D) None of these

4. **What is the perimeter of the given figure?**

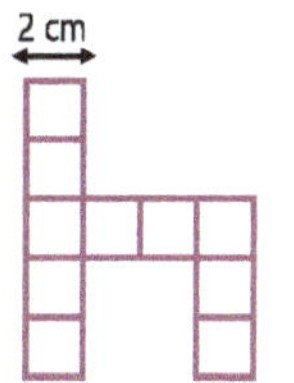

   A) 48 cm   B) 44 cm

   C) 42 cm   D) 46 cm

5. **In the given diagram, what is the least number of triangles that must be shaded so that the given figure is symmetrical along the dotted line?**

   A) 2   B) 1

   C) 4   D) 2

6. **How many rectangles are there in the given figure?**

   A) 4   B) 9

   C) 8   D) 5

7. **Find the length of GH.**

   A) 5 cm   B) 3 cm

   C) 9 cm   D) 1 cm

8. **Which of the following figures has the highest perimeter?**

   A) II

   B) I

   C) III

   D) Can't be determined

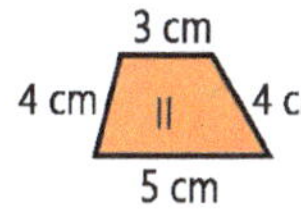

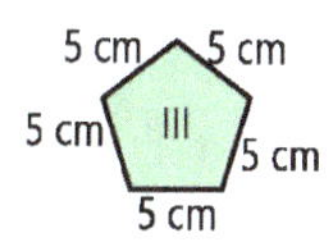

9. **Which line in the diagram is the correct line of symmetry?**

   A) CD   B) AD

   C) EF   D) GH

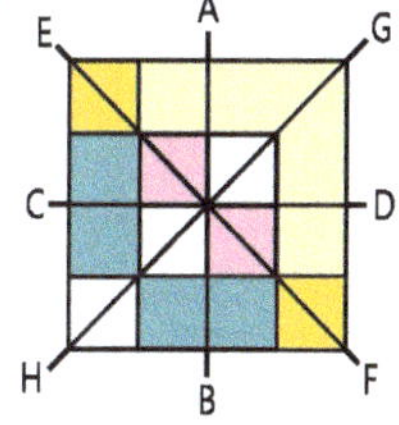

10. **IJKL and MNOP are two squres. Find the length pf KP.**

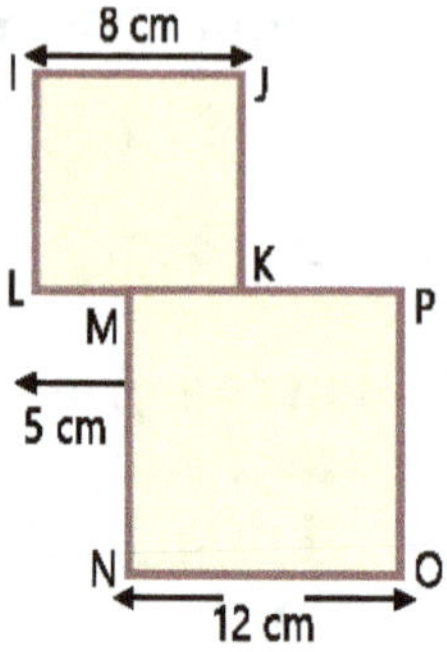

    A) 6 cm

    B) 4 cm

    C) 7 cm

    D) 9 cm

11. **Line p and four points are shown on the grid. Which two points appear to lie on the same line that is parallel to line p?**

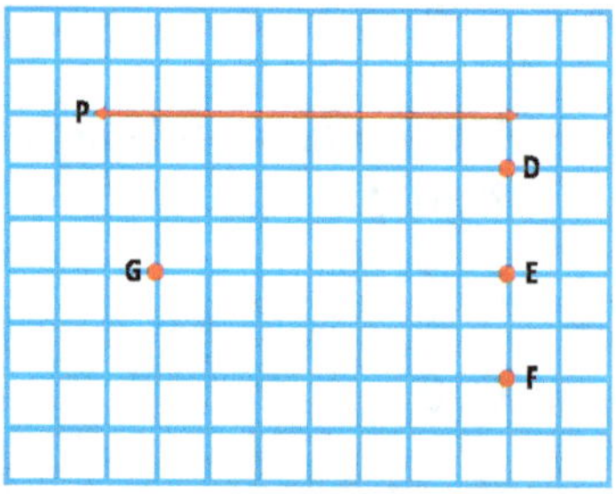

    A) D and E

    B) F and D

    C) G and E

    D) G and D

12. **The triangles shown here was cut into three pieces. Which of the following groups CAN be the three preces of the triangles?**

    A)

    B)

    C)

    D)

13. **The perimeters of triangles X and rectangle Y are equal. Find the lenght of rectangle Y.**

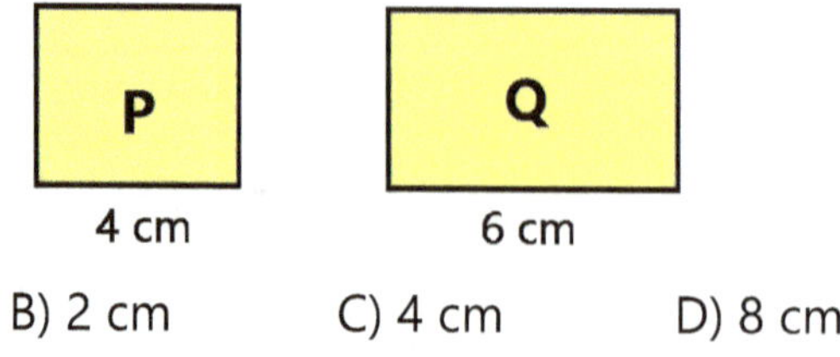

    A) 5 cm   B) 2 cm   C) 4 cm   D) 8 cm

14. **Avi plotted 3 points on a grid line. The three points together make a____.**

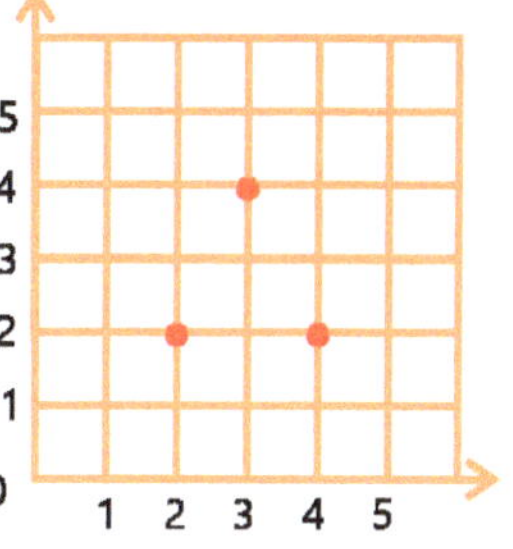

A) Triangle

B) Square

C) Straight line

D) None of these

15. **How many boxes are needed to make the given sold?**

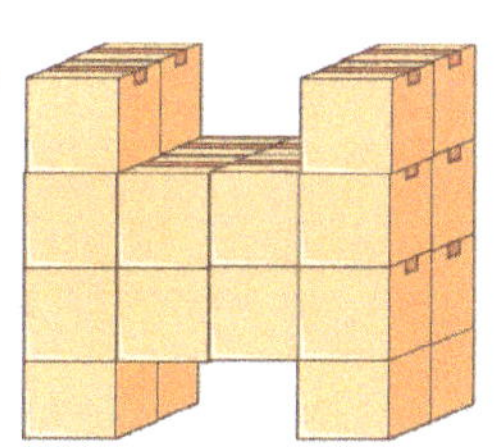

A) 21   B) 24

C) 19   D) 22

16. **Find the perimeter of the shaded part of the given figure.**

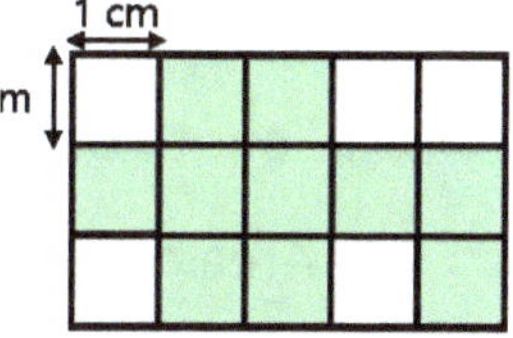

A) 10 cm   B) 12 cm

C) 15 cm   D) 18 cm

17. **Which of the following figures have a line of symmetry?**

A) 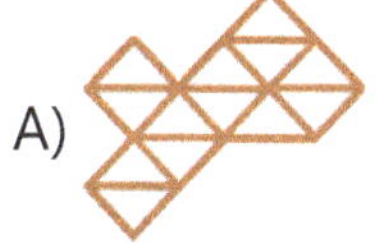   B)    C)    D) 

18. **Study the given graph. Which of the given figures show pair of parallel lines?**

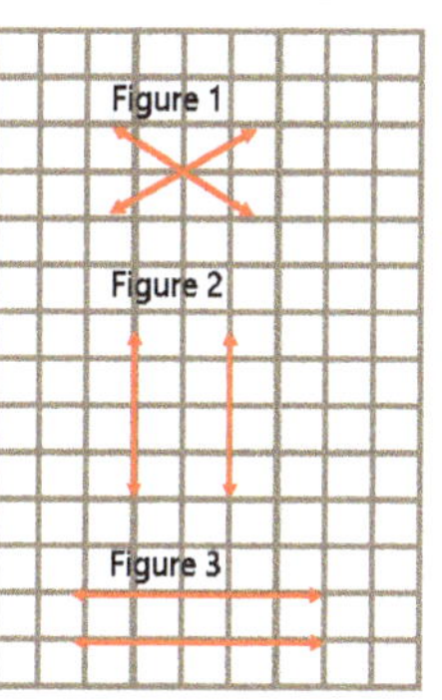

A) Figure 1 and 2

B) Figure 2 and 3

C) Figure 1 and 3

D) None of these

19. **Find the perimeter of the given figure.**

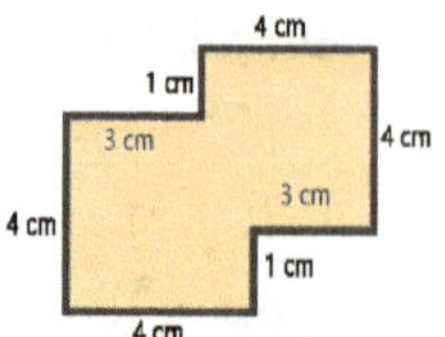

A) 19 cm   B) 22 cm

C) 20 cm   D) 24 cm

20. **Which of the following figures consists of exactly 5 faces?**

A) 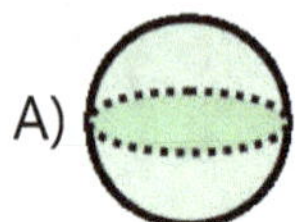   B) 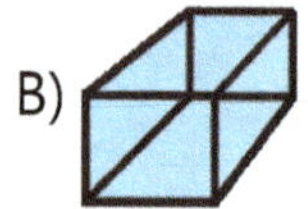   C) 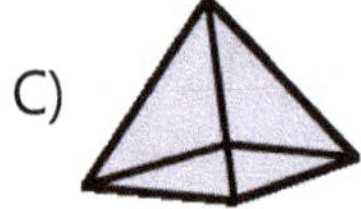   D) 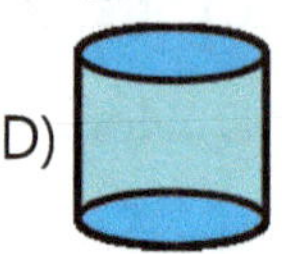

EVERYDAY MATHEMATICS

21. **Rohan plans to cover the boundary of a garden with tiles. What should Rohan know to make sure he buys enough tiles?**

A) Length of garden   B) The perimeter of the garden

C) Area of garden   D) None of these

22. **Anil made a shape by folding the given cardboard along dotted line.**

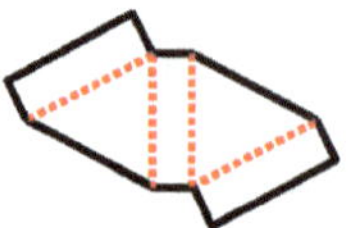

Which shape did Anil make?

A) 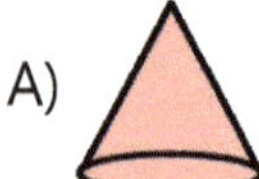   B) 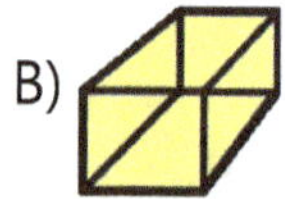   C)    D) 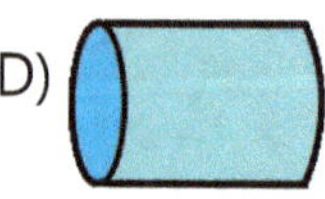

23. **Atul has a field in the shape of rectangle. The length of the field is twice its breadth. The breadth is 80 m. Find the perimeter of the field.**

A) 370 m   B) 480 m   C) 480 m   D) 550 m

24. **An snail is crawling from point A to pint B using the zig zag path. How much distance will it crawl to reach point B?**

A) 14 m   B) 38 m

C) 9 m   D) 11 m

25. **For a design Disha cut a piece of cloth into a shape with 4 sides, but none of them are of the same length. What is the shape of the cloth?**

A) Rectangle   B) Quadrilateral C) Square   D) Pentagon

ACHIEVERS SECTION (HOTS)

26. **The given figure (not drawn to scale) is made up to 6 identical square. The perimeter of the figure is 126 cm. What is the length of each side of the square?**

A) 10 cm   B) 9 cm

C) 6 cm   D) 12 cm

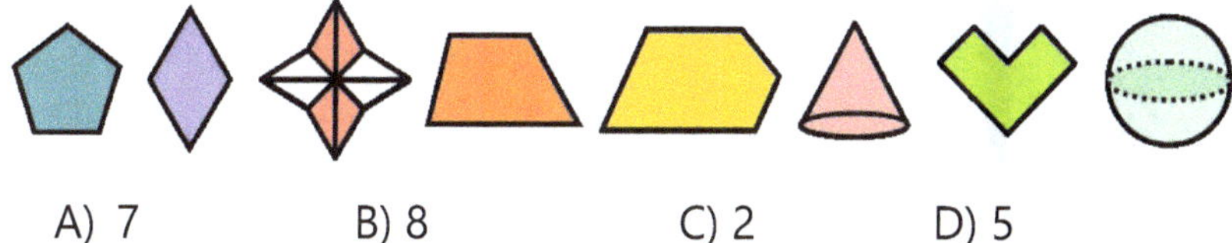

27. **How many of the following figures are not symmetrical?**

A) 7   B) 8   C) 2   D) 5

28. **The given figure of obtained by piecing a rectangle on top of another identical rectangle. The length of a rectangle is 5 cm and its breadth is 2 cm. Find the perimeter of the figure.**

A) 20 cm   B) 18 cm

C) 15 cm   D) 14 cm

29. **Each of the figures below is made up of 2 cm identical squares. Which one of the figures has the greatest perimeter?**

A) 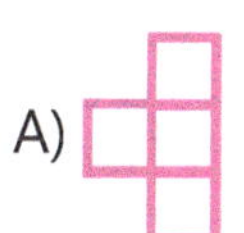   B) 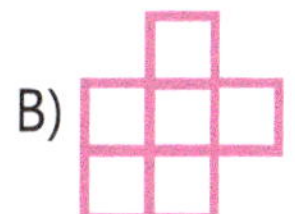   C) 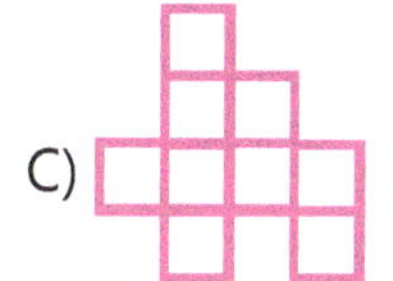   D) 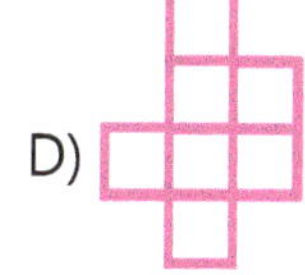

30. **The given figure (not drawn to scale) is made up of a rectangle, a pentagun and a triangle. Find the perimeter of the figure.**

A) 82 cm

B) 85 cm

C) 70 cm

D) 82 cm

<table>
<tr><td colspan="5">Colour your choice with color pencil</td></tr>
<tr><td>1</td><td>2</td><td>3</td><td>4</td><td>5</td></tr>
<tr><td>A B C D</td><td>A B C D</td><td>A B C D</td><td>A B C D</td><td>A B C D</td></tr>
<tr><td>6</td><td>7</td><td>8</td><td>9</td><td>10</td></tr>
<tr><td>A B C D</td><td>A B C D</td><td>A B C D</td><td>A B C D</td><td>A B C D</td></tr>
<tr><td>11</td><td>12</td><td>13</td><td>14</td><td>15</td></tr>
<tr><td>A B C D</td><td>A B C D</td><td>A B C D</td><td>A B C D</td><td>A B C D</td></tr>
<tr><td>16</td><td>17</td><td>18</td><td>19</td><td>20</td></tr>
<tr><td>A B C D</td><td>A B C D</td><td>A B C D</td><td>A B C D</td><td>A B C D</td></tr>
<tr><td>21</td><td>22</td><td>23</td><td>24</td><td>25</td></tr>
<tr><td>A B C D</td><td>A B C D</td><td>A B C D</td><td>A B C D</td><td>A B C D</td></tr>
<tr><td>26</td><td>27</td><td>28</td><td>29</td><td>30</td></tr>
<tr><td>A B C D</td><td>A B C D</td><td>A B C D</td><td>A B C D</td><td>A B C D</td></tr>
</table>

DATA HANDLING

**DO YOU KNOW
WHAT TOPICS WE WILL COVER IN THIS CHAPTER?**

Yes! the topics are;
* Answer the question using information in pictograph or picture graph
* Answer the questions using given bar graphs

MATHEMATICAL REASONING

DIRECTION (1-3): The given pictograph tells us about the kind of games Mayur has play. study the pictograph carefully and answer the following questions.

Games Mayur has played	
Adventures	🎮 🎮 🎮 🎮
Fantasy	🎮 🎮 🎮 🎮
Horror	🎮
Mystery	🎮 🎮 🎮 🎮
Detective	🎮 🎮 🎮 🎮 🎮
One 🎮 equal 4 games	

1. How many games did Mayur play in all?

   A) 84   B) 81   C) 72   D) 75

2. How many detective games did he play?

   A) 22   B) 27   C) 20   D) 19

3. **How many Fantasy games did he play?**

A) 16   B) 22   C) 27   D) 25

DIRECTION (4-6): The following table shows the number of bags sold by factories over a period of 4 months.

	Company P	Company Q	Company R	Company S
January	2545	2254	1000	900
February	1268	1393	1217	1218
March	1864	1900	1354	1305
April	2154	2387	1747	983

4. **How many bags did company P sell in these 4 months?**

A) 7831   B) 7835   C) 7843   D) 7854

5. **How many bags did company Q sell more than company R in January and February altogether?**

A) 1425   B) 1433   C) 1430   D) 1445

6. **Find the number of bags company S and company R sold in these 4 months altogether.**

A) 9783   B) 9755   C) 9733   D) 9724

DIRECTION (7-9): Study the graph and answer the following questions.

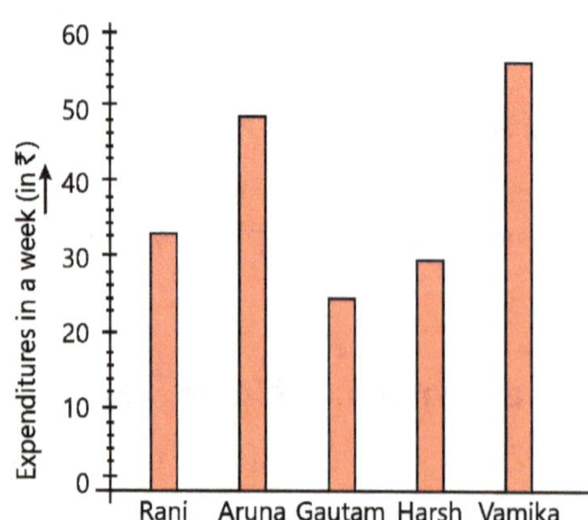

7. **How much money must Aruna give to Gautam so that both of them will have the same amount of money?**

   A) ₹ 12   B) ₹ 22   C) ₹ 18   D) ₹ 33

8. **How much money all the five friends spend in the week?**

   A) ₹ 58   B) ₹ 180   C) ₹ 270   D) ₹ 90

9. **How much less money did harsh spend than remaining four friends altogether?**

   A) ₹ 150   B) ₹ 160   C) ₹ 190   D) ₹ 250

DIRECTION (10-12): The bar graph shows the types of sports students like.

10. **____ more people like Basketball than swimming.**

    A) 9   B) 3   C) 5   D) 7

11. **7 less people prefer cycling than ___.**

    A) badminton   B) Jogging   C) Cricket   D) Basketball

12. **The total number of people who like basketball and __ is 42.**

    A) Baskrtball   B) Cycling   C) Crickrt   D) Jogging

DIRECTION (13-15): Study the graph and answer the following question.

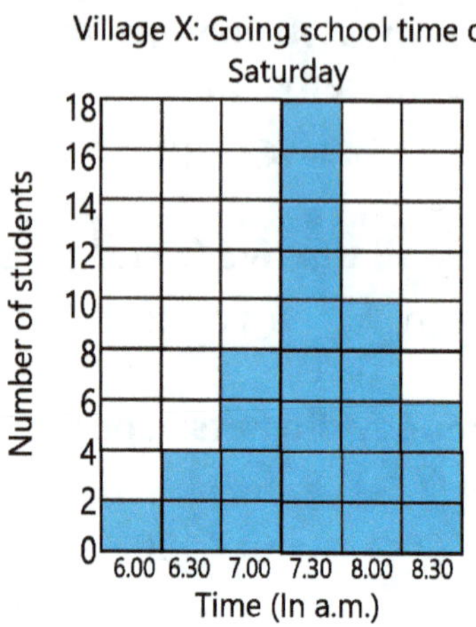

13. **At what time most students going to school on saturday morning?**

A) 7.30 a.m   B) 8.30 a.m   C) 6.00 a.m   D) 60.30 a.m

14. **How many students going to school at 6:30 a.m?**

A) 2   B) 3   C) 4   D) 7

15. **How many students going to school during the period from 7:00 and to 8:00 a.m?**

A) 17   B) 36   C) 44   D) 29

DIRECTION (16-19): The bar graph shows Arun's profit from Jun to October.

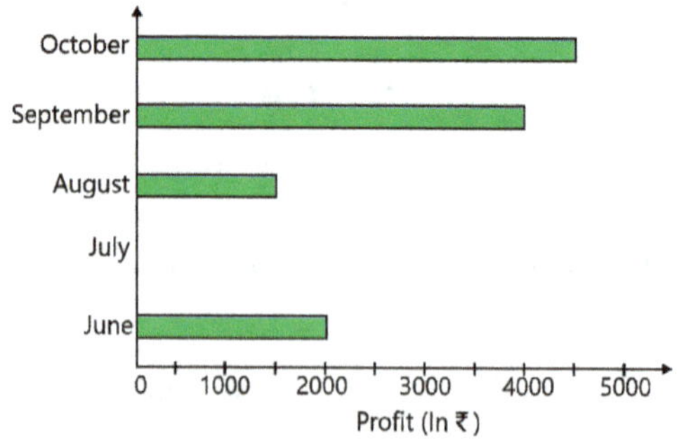

16. **How much more did Arun profit in September than in August?**

A) ₹ 2500   B) ₹ 2300   C) ₹ 3500   D) ₹ 3000

17. **If Arun earn a total of ₹ 15000 from Jully to October, then how much did he earn in Jully?**

    A) ₹ 2500   B) ₹ 4000   C) ₹ 3000   D) ₹ 3500

18. **In which month did Arun earn thrice the amount of money saved in August?**

    A) October   B) Jun   C) Jully   D) August

19. **If Arun spent $\left(\frac{1}{5}\right)^{th}$ of the amount of money he earn in September, then how much he earned in that month?**

    A) ₹ 3400   B) ₹ 900   C) ₹ 4800   D) ₹ 4200

DIRECTION (20-22): The given shows the number of computers sold by Ashish computer mart over 5 months. Study the graph and answer the following questions.

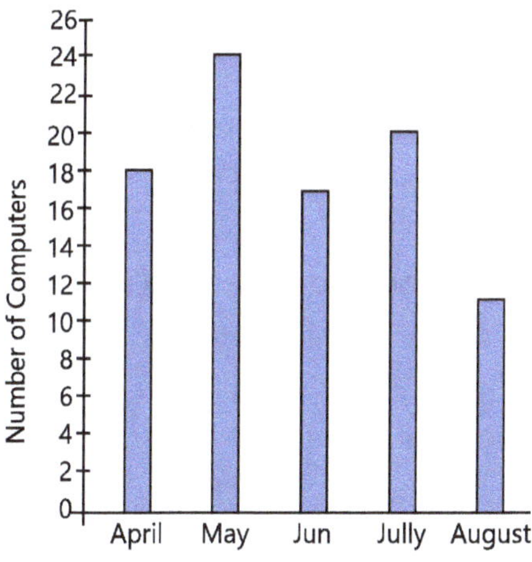

20. **In which month was there the biggest increase in the number of computers sold?**

    A) Jully   B) April   C) May   D) Jun

21. **If each computers costs ₹ 250, then how much less did Ashish computer mart collect in August than in Jully?**

A) ₹ 2000   B) ₹ 2500   C) ₹ 3000   D) ₹ 1500

22. **What was the total sale of computers for Ashish computer mart during the five months?**

    A) 90   B) 40   C) 55   D) 60

DIRECTION (23-25): The given graph shows the number of books sale by 6 shops in May. Study the graph and answer the following question.

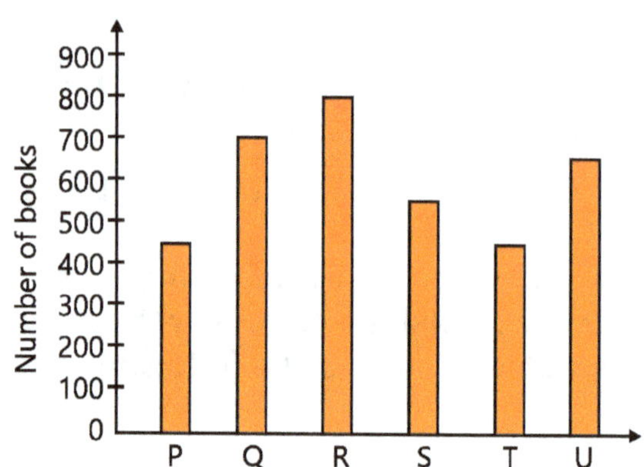

23. **Which shop sold 250 more books than shop P?**

    A) Q   B) R   C) T   D) U

24. **How many more books did shop Q sell than shop U?**

    A) 50   B) 80   C) 140   D) 200

25. **How many books did the 6 shops sell altogether?**

    A) 3050   B) 3600   C) 3450   D) 3700

ACHIEVERS SECTION (HOTS)

26. **The given graph shows the number of participants that were present at each event of School games.**

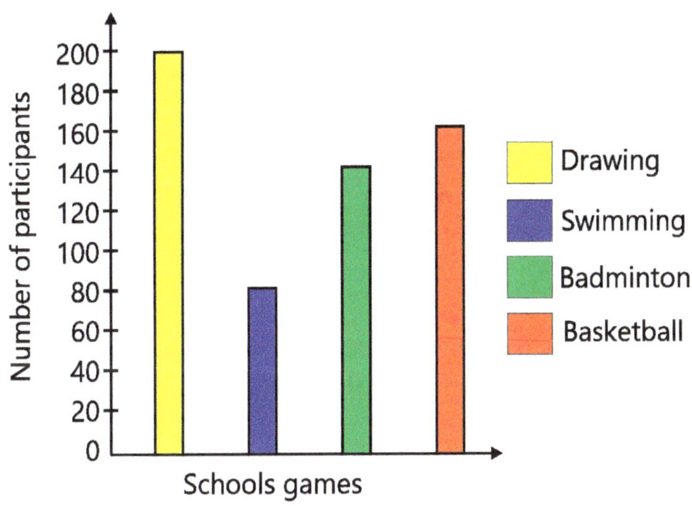

The difference between the maximum and minimum number of participants in these events is____.

A) 110   B) 70   C) 50   D) 120

27. **The given graph shows the number of viewers to watch the movies during a four month period.**

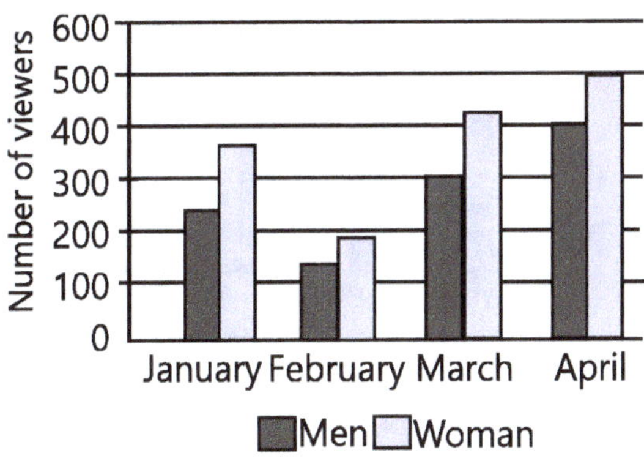

In which month is there $1\frac{1}{5}$ times as many viewers as in January?

A) Febuary   B) March   C) April   D) January

28. **The given table shows the number of people who joined a cricket club in 2019 and 2020.**

Years People	2019	2020
Men	3205	2804
Women	4809	6408
Boys	1600	2000
Girls	2405	1807

What was the difference in the number of men who joined the cricket club between 2019 and 2020?

A) 980   B) 1599   C) 401   D) 1607

29. **The given graph shows the sales of a factory from Wenesday to Sunday.**

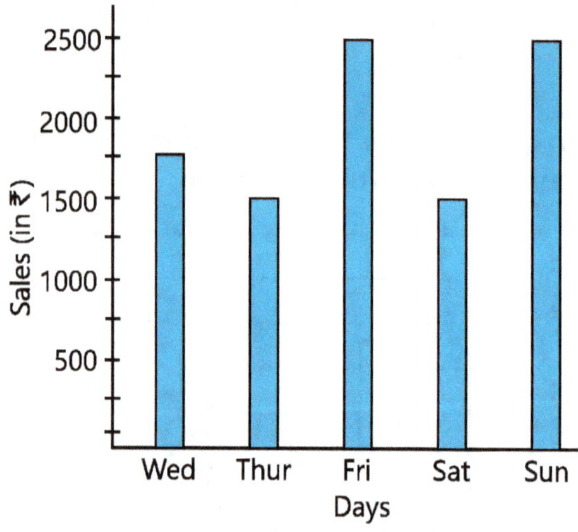

If the sales made a Monday was $1\frac{3}{4}$ times the total sales made on Saturday and Friday, then how much sales was made on Sunday?

A) ₹ 2540   B) ₹ 2500   C) ₹ 4580   D) ₹ 7000

30. **The given bar graph shows the savings (in ₹) of five workers.**

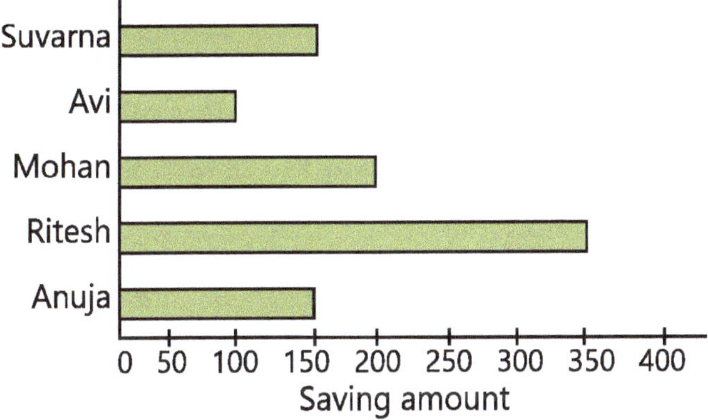

Ritesh needs to save another___ so that he has twice as much money as Mohan.

A) ₹ 50　　　B) ₹ 200　　　C) ₹ 150　　　D) ₹ 250

CHAPTER 7

LOGICAL REASONING

DO YOU KNOW
WHAT TOPICS WE WILL COVER IN THIS CHAPTER?

Yes! the topics are;

* Patterns: (i) Number patterns (ii) Figure patterns
* Analogy: Comparing two pairs of given figures or terms
* Odd One Out: Identify the odd term, figure or object amongest the given terms figures or objects
* Embedded Figures
* Mirror Images
* Alphabet text
* Direction Sense test
* Ranking Test: Finding the position of a termor a object from the given position
* Coding-Decoding
* Geometrical Shapes and Solids
* Days & Dates and Possible Combinations

MATHEMATICAL REASONING

1. **Select figure from the operations which when placed in blanks space of Fig.(X) would complete the pattern.**

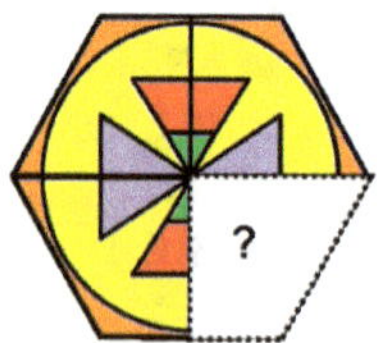

Fig. (X)

 A)
 B)
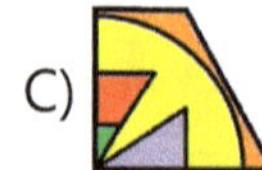 C)
 D)

2. **The positions of the first and the second digits in the number 83726415 are interchanged. Similarly, the positions of the**

third and fourth digits are interchanged and so on. Which of the following will be the third to the left of the seventh digit from the left after the rearrangement?

A) 8   B) 2   C) 3   D) 7

3. Parth is facing towards north. He makes $\frac{3}{4}$ turn to his right and then $\frac{1}{2}$ turn In pond direction. Now If he wants to face towards the pond, then what turn will he make from the given options?

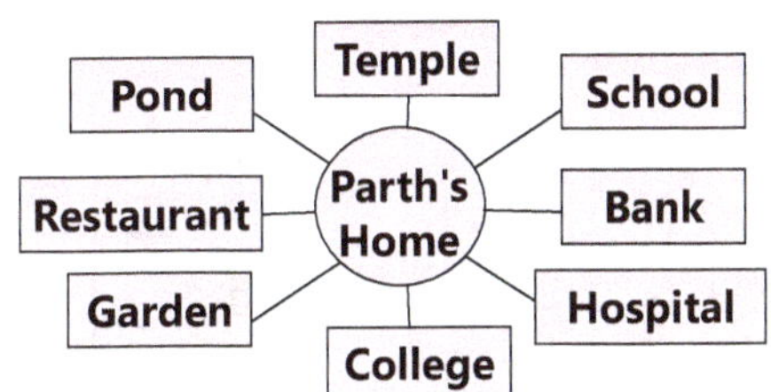

A) $\frac{1}{4}$ turn anticlockwise   B) $\frac{5}{8}$ turn clockwise

C) $\frac{3}{4}$ turn towards right   D) $\frac{7}{8}$ turn towards left

DIRECTION (4-5): There is a certain relationship between fig.(i) and (ii). Establish a similar relationship between fig. (iii) and (iv) by selecting a figure from the options which will replace the (?) in the fig.(iv).

4.
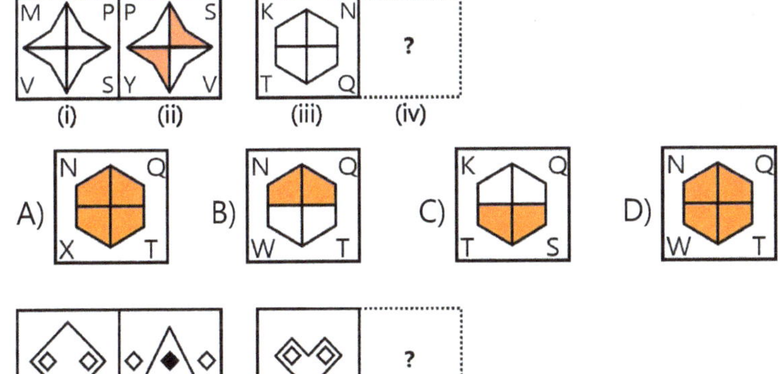

5.
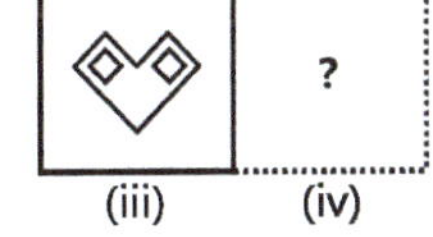

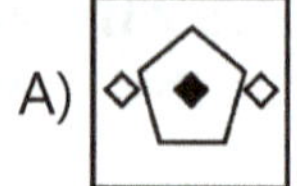  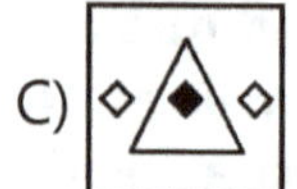 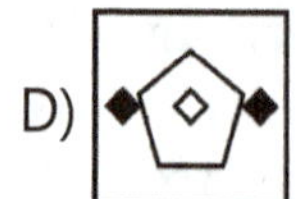

DIRECTION (6-7): Which of the following is the CORRECT miror image of fig.(X). If mirror is placed along PQ?

6.

A) 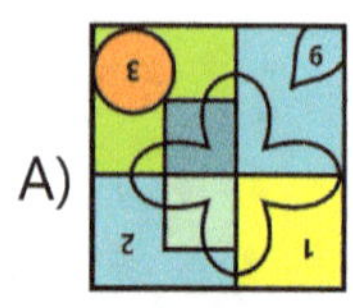 B)  C) 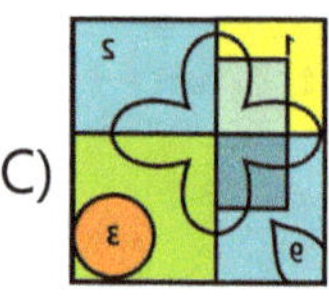 D) 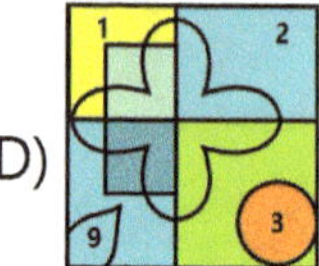

7.

Fig. (X)

A) 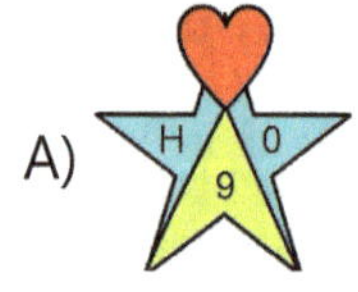 B)  C) 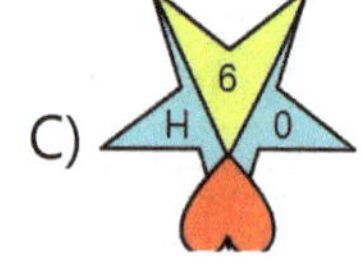 D) 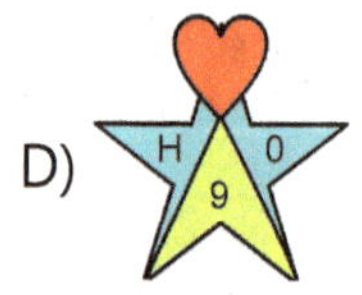

8. **If the given clock is 30 minutes fast, then the CORRECT time after one an hour will be___**

A) 4 O' Clock

B) 4 : 30

C) 5 O' Clock

D) 5 : 30

9. **Which of the following figures will continue the given problem figure?**

Problem Figure

A)   B)   C)   D)

10. **Select the CORRECT match.**

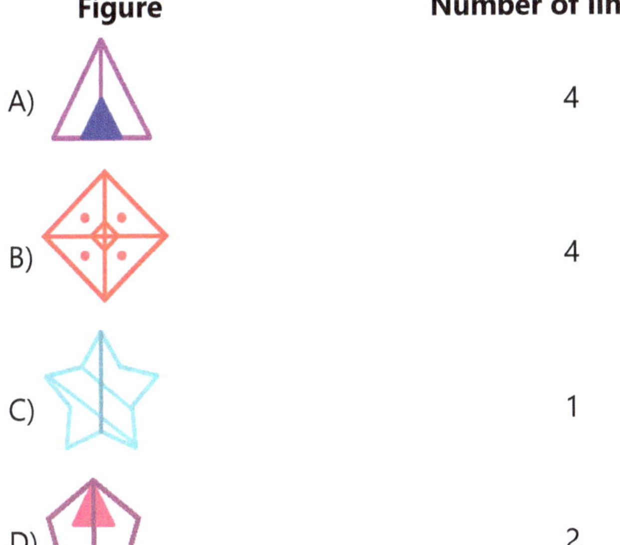

Figure	Number of line symmetry
A)	4
B)	4
C)	1
D)	2

11. **Given below is the unfolded from of paper. Which of the following is the CORRECT figure when the paper is folded along the dotted line?**

A)   B)   C)   D)

12. **Select a number from the options which will replace the question mark, if a certain rule is followed in the figures.**

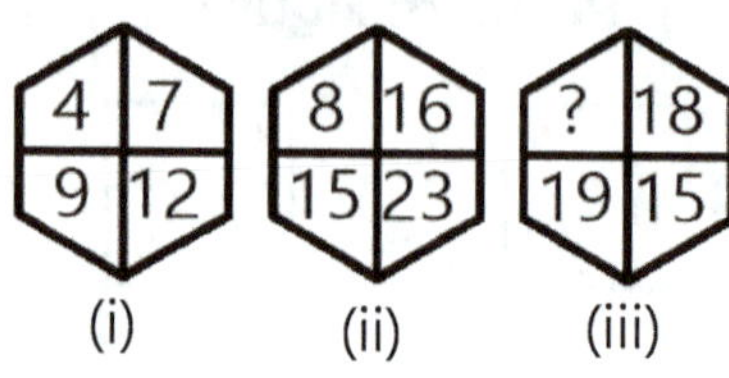

(i)   (ii)   (iii)

A) 22   B) 21   C) 19   D) 15

13. **How many stars are there in the given figure?**

A) 12   B) 10   C) 15   D) 12

14. **Arrange the following words according to dictionary arrangement.**

   1. Pear   2. Pineapple   3. Pappaya

   4. Peach   5. Passionfruit

   A) 1, 2, 3, 4, 5   B) 3, 5, 4, 1, 2

   C) 3, 2, 5, 1, 4   D) 5, 3, 4, 2, 1

15. **Which of the following options is embedded in the given figure (X)?**

A)    B) 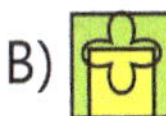   C) 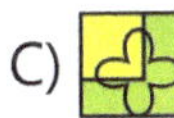   D) 

16. **Some letters are given which are numbered 1,2,3,4,5 and 6 followed by four options containing combinations of these numbers. Find the combination of numbers so that letters arranged accordingly from a meaningful word.**

O E C O H S

1 2 3 4 5 6

A) 4, 3, 5, 6, 1, 2   B) 2, 3, 5, 1, 4, 6

C) 3, 2, 4, 1, 5, 6   D) 3, 5, 1, 4, 6, 2

17. **Deepesh's exam start just after 4th Friday of August 20XX. The date on which Deepesh exam start is___**

August 20XX						
Mon	Tue	Wed	Thu	Fri	Sat	Sun
	1	2	3	4	5	6
7	8	9	10	11	12	13
14	15	16	17	18	19	20
21	22	23	24	25	26	27
28	29	30	31			

A) 26th August   B) 26th August

C) 4th August   D) 31st August

18. **Select the odd one out.**

A) 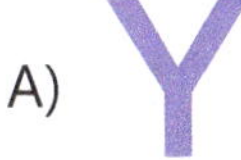   B)    C)    D) F

19.. **If 'pen' is called 'eraser', 'eraser' is called 'shapner', 'shapner' is called 'book' and 'book' is called 'ruller', then if Kavya is writting some letters what would she used?**

A) Eraser   B) Pen   C) Sharpner   D) Book

20. **If SNAKE is written as @#?&% And PLANE is written as ©*?#%, then how will LAKE be written?**

A) @?#%   B) *?&%   C) ©*?*%   D) @*?#&

21. **Which of the following is the lightest Weight?**

A) 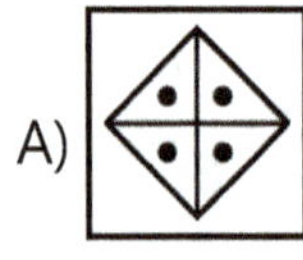   B) 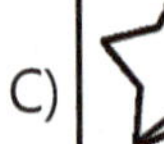   C) 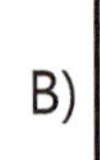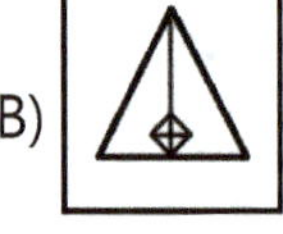   D) Can't be determined

22. **Anil is taller than the Atul. Nitin is taller than Anil but similar than the Manoj. Which of the following is the CORRECT order of height from the tallest to the shortest?**

A) Atul, Anil, Manoj, Nitin   B) Manoj, Atul, Anil, Nitin

C) Anil, Nitin, Manoj, Atul   D) Manoj, Nitin, Anil, Atul

DIRECTION (23-24): In which of the following options, Fig. (X) is not embedded as one if its part.

23. **Images Fig. (X)**

Fig. (X)

24. **Images Fig. (X)**

A) 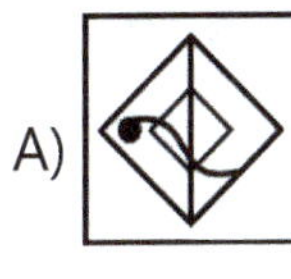

C) 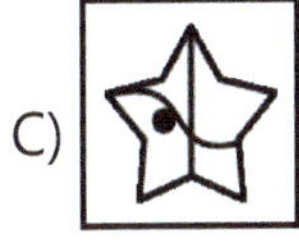

B) 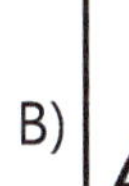

D) 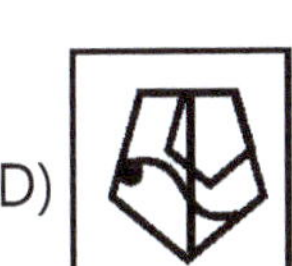

Fig. (X)

25. **Which of the following numbers will continue the given series?**

50, 48, 44, 38, 30?

A) 24　　　B) 20　　　C) 22　　　D) 18

26. **If the day after tomorrow was Monday, then what day will be day before yesterday?**

A) Thursday　　B) Monday　　C) Friday　　D) Sunday

27. **In a play competition, there are 5 finalists.**

Sahil: He is just after Ritesh.

Shubham: He has only one boy behind his.

Aman: He is just before Shubham.

Tarun: He is not the first.

__and__ stood at first and last positions respectively

A) Sahil, Ritesh　　　　B) Ritesh, Tarun

C) Sahil, Aman　　　　D) Aman, Tarun

28. **How many squres are there in the given figure?**

A) 11

B) 10

C) 12

D) 13

29. **Arya walks towards east. After walking some distance, she take a right turn and again walking some distance she take a left turn. In which direction she will be facing now?**

A) West   B) South   C) East   D) North

30. **How many possible combinations of 1 bottle and 1 glass can be formed from 5 bottles and 3 glasses?**

A) 10   B) 18   C) 12   D) 15

www.ingramcontent.com/pod-product-compliance
Lightning Source LLC
LaVergne TN
LVHW050543200726
843506LV00001B/74